Searching For The Sunset

Alex Ramsden

BookLeaf Publishing

Presentation by *BookLeaf Publishing*

Web: www.bookleafpub.com

E-mail: info@bookleafpub.com

ISBN: 9789357213134

First edition 2023

4 a.m.

Every day would be perfect if it were spent with
you
No star in the universe shines as brightly as
those eyes
When I tell you I love you, and you say it too
If our love was in a raffle, it would be the first
prize.

But now this has got all cute and soppy
Like summat that Shakespeare would write
I'm better than him, though, he's a weed and I'm
a poppy
And I'm writing this at 4am, I should probably
call it a night.

The Worst Five Minutes of My Love Life

I don't know what drove you to do it
Maybe it was fate
You burned my jacket with matches
And then slammed the gate
You left me a glowering inferno
I put it out with my tears
Rain from my eyes so subtle
With your voice ringing in my ears

There were times I really loved you
Looking back is no mistake
Its barely been a year now
Still I don't feel awake
We argued and loved and smiled
Our hearts on fire together
With beats missing
We were out of sync forever

Maybe it was time for me to go
The sun shone down on my face

Then came the clouds
And I was lost in a lonely place
Without you was never an option
Interlocked through space and time
I guess that's what they call the blues
Running down the grapevine.

The Friend Zone

Making you happy
Was like climbing a mountain
And always getting stuck at base camp.

Making you satisfied
Was like being stuck in traffic
From here to the moon and stars.

Making you mine
Was like a black and white rainbow
Pointless, fruitless and useless.

Embarrassment in the Supermarket

I went to the checkout with my anxiety nagging
An unexpected item in bagging!!!!!!!
The girl at the checkout, cheerful and sweet
Laughing as I awkwardly look at my feet,
Asks if I need help packing?
My bag for life seriously lacking!
I've fallen head over heels…
Laden down with microwave meals…
I leave with a smile, a look, a flirt.
Only to notice I had a stain down my shirt.

December

The trees are bare, the snow is on the ground
You don't have to be cold, I'll be around
Wrapped up in each other, away from the chill
The late-night sky, so silent, so still
Lighting a fire, you laughed when it went out
With that sulky face I love, the one I can't be
without
I kissed you tenderly, melting in the heat
Our romance gave light to the whole street
The bleak winter thawed under you and me
December was our time to be free.

The fire burns out, slowly by dying ember
Forget summer, the cuddly embrace of
December
Was better than everything else. It was ours
It was nothing else as spring cowers
The freezing air, we shared together those days
In loving bliss, with each glance and gaze
There was nothing to stop us, or put out that fire
With tinsel and holly and a festive choir
My favourite place to be, it's true
Is anywhere, December, with you.

Taxis at Twilight

The shadows of the pale, morning sun
Pigeons plucking scraps from the night
Off the floor where leather and laces have run
The thin sky guiding taxis at twilight.

A carousel plays out in clouds of colour
The distant thrum of early-doors traffic
The blue in the air is full and getting fuller
Against remaining dark, grasping and graphic.

The long and lucid soliloquy of meandering drunks
Waylaid from home, rolling stones and stoned
The familiar sound of the milk float clunks
An age of early starts professionally honed.

The streets are dull and softly flat
A call from the seagull's punches through silence
Broken glass and a shrill, shrieking cat
The hangover of the previous night's violence.

The sun finally bursts through, powerful and strong
Yet so far away as burden meets birdsong

It doesn’t take long
To feel that this is the path we truly belong.

The Beautiful Game

As you approach, there's the roar of the crowd
Been like that forever, yet you're still proud
This football lark, nothing compares
To a feeling of defeat or trophies upstairs
The belonging and family in the stand
If you fall down, they'd lend a hand
The laminated ball means everything to you
Some say it's sad, others think how you do
Nothing beats the swaying support
All in the name of this national sport
Only football can truly break your heart
But you will always feel like you are a part
Forget the violent, drunken reputation
Thrust upon us by this great nation
You are a football fan, you are part of it all
You are the barmy army, following that ball
As the soundtrack rocks to Britpop and bass
The sting of a wet ball in your face
You'd never change any part of it, though
Trust me on that one, I know.

Sweets

The strawberry sunshine in her eyes
The citrus clouds of sweet and sour
The scent of the flowers
Chocolate conversations for hours
How to make sense of this life?

The tinge of tangy love
The spray of the nectar
The cinnamon explosion of sex
Made to measure in a vanilla vortex.
How to make sense of this life?

The exciting gloop of custard dreams
The crumble of the gooey morning
The smiling face of sticky angel lips
Swinging from the tropical hips
How to make sense of this life?

The decadent touch of velvety hands
The delicate nibble of marzipan ear lobes
The dripping defiance of a dozen nights
Spent holding onto candied sights:
How to make sense of this life?

Enjoy The Ride (Scream If You Wanna Go Faster)

For every raindrop, there can be a rainbow.
For every glaring miss, there are subtle victories.
For every nothing, there is an everything.
For every painful break, there can be hope.

Life follows no pattern,
It changes tense,
Makes little sense,
Sometimes seems a pretence,
It is volatile and intense,
A mix of concrete and essence.

For every slippery floor, there is a solution.
For every day of pain, there are weeks of love.
For every moment of madness, there can be sanity.
For every sad death, there is happy rebirth.

Life is one long daydream,
A trip through the soul,

Discovering the journey and the role,
An endless quest towards the goal,
As part of the glistening shoal,
With billions of parts making a whole.

For every delusion, there is destiny.
For every heart, there is a partner.
For every footstep, there is life.
For every show of passion, there is poetry.

On A Cold, Wintry Night

On a cold, wintry night,
The trees whistle in the wind,
The sky is sullen and black,
A mood as macabre as Lovecraft .
Every noise, sounds insignificant,
Yet makes a crescendo in the darkness,
An arpeggio of chirrups and chirps,
A creaking, squeaking symphony; soft and slow.

On a cold, wintry night,
The moon is obscured in the clouds,
Grey wisps of candied bliss cover the orb,
A shrill, shadow of silver.
Every star burning through the galaxy,
Its heat a million miles away,
Lighting the glisten of the groaning grass,
Nocturnal feet scamper in the shuffling shore.

On a cold, wintry night,
The chilling breeze flutters,
It slams rocks and shakes meadows,
The waves in the distance break in a hush.

On a cold, wintry night,
The smell of the rain mingles,
An atmosphere of lunar solemnity,
Watched by endless light-years and lighthouses.

On a cold, wintry night,
The mind ponders the fresh air,
The ears redden in the biting blow,
The mouth billows breath like a chimney.
On a cold, wintry night,
Nature stays awake,
The frost lies in wait,
For the morning after the cold, wintry night.

Nothing Left To Save

There's nothing left to save
Nothing worth keeping as a memento
A domino effect of empty luck, we gave
A promise of treasure and love.
Forlorn, it passed through stages of time
Settling like seltzer in the stomach
At the end of the line
This emphatic stop sign of a memory.
A chorus of sweet mystery in surround
A bright and clear morning to savour
Hatred and regret take off from the ground
The clamour and clash of a clean break.
A moment in life, manipulated and lost
An origami of broken contentment
Stuck forever in reverse, decline, perma-frost
When there's nothing left to save.

WWW.

Everyone is on their smart phones these days
Everyone feels the need to join in a craze
Social media, technology and the quest for peace
Enslaving the human race piece by piece

Everyone tries to get involved in the maze
Candies crushed and maybe, I'm amazed
By the power of the web and the written word
Sharing, liking, downloading unperturbed.

October Sky

It's that time of year
The leaves go golden
Red and yellow;
The sky turns black
Rain, wind, swirling
Biting until you shed a tear

The autumnal feeling
Wet, drab and dying
The cold snap soon;
Warm fireplaces
Gloves and coats
And pots of hot darjeeling

Sodden grass
Threadbare trees
Rotting leaves;
Steamed up windows
Puddles underfoot
The power of the season's mass.

Living on the 'B' Side

I travelled far and wide to bring forth this tale
Of times past, all forgotten and stale
The weapons of truth, love and victory
All mixed in with guilt, betrayal and ecstasy

The battles that had ensued
Gettysburg, St Petersburg, Battenberg, Henning Berg
A ship cast adrift in a sea of trouble
As all around it falls a mass of rubble

We played there and took the away end
The Stretford, Clock and Brummie Bend
We swarmed all over the charming seaside
And to a soundtrack of the brilliant 'B' side

The Californian bombshell in our midst
Everyone tried it on while pissed
Don't come out on the lash with the lads
If you can't handle the laughs and the cads

I found myself stuck in Nantwich

Or was it Middlewich, Northwich or Norwich?
I couldn't tell which 'wich' was which
So I stood on the motorway waiting to hitch

Dancing to punk and funk
As we prepared to clunk and bunk
A wandering star has no boss
As a rolling stone gathers no moss

This story of confusion and illusion
Morphs into revolution and allusion
Did all this stuff really take place?
Or did you imagine it in time, in space.

A Dis-United Kingdom

There are some things that should never be
Circus clowns, cannons and camaraderie
As milk goes sour in the doorway
Whilst training dogs to sit and stay.
The forgotten youths hang round outside shops
Terrorising people and running from cops
Reebok classics, hoodies and bikes
All with no future, all on strike.
People getting married for summat to do
Something old, something borrowed, and blue
The TV tells us what to think
Only on Points of View can you kick up a stink.
Staffy dogs, fat people and fast food
Developing a 'so what' attitude
Nothing matters, everything is shit
Is it so hard to rise out from your pit?
The morning sun casts light on the town
The sound of seagulls and the smell of brown
As junkies sleep, milkmen awake
They work every day, never get a break.
Alcohol, ASBOs and arson
Calling the waiter Garcon

The beggars busking for money
As passers-by call them a 'rummy'.
This is England, in so few words
Visit the estates, with their herds
Rascals, robbers and rags
The streets littered with plastic bags.
The same story, different city
Weather warnings and nothing is pretty
Huge waist bands, huge benefits
Politicians don't care, the shits.
As time goes by, it gets worse
As time goes on, so does the curse
Vandals, graffiti and crime
All ahead of it's time.
A failure as a community
Political immunity
These are the things that make me mad
Are things really that bad?

A Heart Made of Honey

A heart made of honey, lungs breathing sunshine
Holding safely in our sleep, dreams bordering on the sublime
There is affection in those eyes, beautiful and blue
Smiling passion from the lashes, false, but also true.

My rock in a storm, sheltering from pain
A feeling from the soles of my feet to the soul of my brain
A smile crafted from beauty, from hope
Looking over the horizon together, with our telescope.

I Don't Wanna Know

Sitting in the shade
Listening to the lapping waves
I don’t wanna know how the world behaves

Soaking up the sun
Watching the light bounce on the sea
I don’t wanna know anything except you and me

Singing through the storm
The rain making puddles of chrome
I don’t wanna know if they plot the way home

Sleeping by the stars
A canvas of love and hope in panoramic vision
I don’t wanna know about the right or wrong
decision.

A Long, Long Way From Home

My tongue got stuck on the words trying to describe
How the rainbow disappeared into a sky of chrome
Your hand in mine, wrapped in ecstasy
A long, long way from home.

The thought of you in my bones
Keeping the heart warm and glowing, moonlight
Shining over the souls of Sunday
Another reflection towards eternal delight.

My tongue got stuck on the words trying to describe
How the rainbow disappeared into a sky of chrome
Your hand in mine, wrapped in ecstasy
A long, long way from home.

The latest chapter in our personal quest
Played out with the ocean between us
On opposite sides of the world we loved

The spies in the window to the heart could never
have seen us.

My tongue got stuck on the words trying to
describe
How the rainbow disappeared into a sky of
chrome
Your hand in mine, wrapped in ecstasy
A long, long way from home.

Saturday Night Story Time

There's smoke floating in your eyes
A scrawl of lyrics snaking up your thigh
Fishnets obscure the view
Of skin dotted with colourful tattoos
We met on a Saturday night
In the bright and breezy spring night
Too many drinks and too many dances
Slippery floors and not taking my chances
Leaned in for a kiss
Signed, sealed, puddles of piss
Deny the delivery of a love scene
Bathed in flashes of envious green.

There's ash flicking over your boots
Midnight in suede, gold in your roots
Conversation stilted in stereo, chronic
The fizz and tang of the fifth gin and tonic
A lingering look into the face, the soul
Dazzled by a dizzying goal
You were the essence of sweet desire
Wrapped up in denim, to admire
Your beautiful smile would be to die

A beautiful death, you were so shy
The comfort of my arms could never be enough
To rescue your tab end from igniting floor fluff.

There's more to love than looks
There are opinions, films, books,
A good and deep discussion
A sweaty and strategically placed cushion
The morning after the night before
The empty takeaway boxes across the floor
A thick and cloying stench of grease
Keys jingling in the pockets of a fleece
Music plays out a luscious love affair
Every dream, every blink, every nightmare
Was worth it for you and worth it for me
I will adore you, always, that's my guarantee.

If It Takes A Village Idiot, Then There Are Plenty of Candidates

Why do I wake up before my alarm clock goes off, to see if my alarm clock is about to go off? What a waste of life.

Some people hate the thought of being married because they like their freedom, but any good marriage has a good wife.

If I could ever live on another planet then it would have to be Mars, where we men come from; but only because Venus would be nagging.

I ask you, menfolk, can we spend millions of pounds a year at Valentine's to keep the woman happy, and then they can go around bragging?

Just stupid things like that annoy me no end, like how am I supposed to know the difference between a handbag and a clutch?

I once tried to get my head round why that certain pair of shoes didn't go with that certain colour dress, it was like Double Dutch .

But, I digress, the vagaries of modern life are becoming such that I feel like we're wading through treacle and losing a shoe.
And that nothing matters more than the latest internet craze, the latest celebrity anorexia scares; and to be honest, I haven't a clue.
As I reach the age of twenty-two, I wanted to express my irritation at the state of the world, the state of my generation.
It is one of smart phones, nicking traffic cones, being a Belieber , video games, name and shames and media saturation.
2021 swept in from out of nowhere, when you can travel through time in fifty years- you'll never want to go back there.

Mediterranean Homebase Blues

Do you know where the power tools are?
What aisle am I looking for, is it far?
Help me with these Mediterranean Homebase Blues.

I can see the D.I.Y men, eyes fixed on the guarantee
Black and Decker in hand, staring straight past me
They can sense that I don't belong
As the testosterone is powerfully strong.

Go back to look at the deck chairs
All stacked neatly in their colourful pairs
Help me with these Mediterranean Homebase Blues.

The polystyrene packaged sander
Middle aged men queuing to have a gander
The shop assistant points me to the tiles
Why do these aisles go on for miles?

The garden centre is full of flowers
And female conversation going on for hours
Talking about Mediterranean Homebase Blues.

I asked a question and looked right at you
"Why is there no cafe, like at B & Q ?"
On closer inspection, it was an elaborate ruse
To help me get over the Mediterranean
Homebase Blues.

www.ingramcontent.com/pod-product-compliance
Lightning Source LLC
Chambersburg PA
CBHW062110140826
49812CB00058B/1157
* 9 7 8 9 3 5 7 2 1 3 1 3 4 *